HR AND TECHNOLOGY: IMPACT AND ADVANTAGES

Dr Emma Parry

Professor Shaun Tyson

Doone Selbie

Ray Leighton

The Chartered Institute of Personnel and Development is the leading publisher of books and reports for personnel and training professionals, students, and all those concerned with the effective management and development of people at work.
For full details of all our titles, please contact the Publishing Department:
Tel: 020 8612 6204
E-mail: publish@cipd.co.uk

To view and purchase all CIPD titles:
www.cipd.co.uk/bookstore

For details of CIPD research projects:
www.cipd.co.uk/research

HR AND TECHNOLOGY: IMPACT AND ADVANTAGES

Dr Emma Parry

Professor Shaun Tyson

HUMAN RESOURCE RESEARCH CENTRE, CRANFIELD SCHOOL OF MANAGEMENT

Doone Selbie

Ray Leighton

First published 2007
Reprinted 2008

Cover and text design by Sutchinda Rangsi-Thompson
Typeset by Paperweight
Printed in Great Britain by Antony Rowe

British Library Cataloguing in Publication Data
A catalogue record for this book is available from the British Library

ISBN-13 978 1 84398 183 1

Chartered Institute of Personnel and Development,
151 The Broadway, London SW19 1JQ

Tel: 020 8612 6200
Website: www.cipd.co.uk

Incorporated by Royal Charter. Registered charity no. 1079797.

CONTENTS

LIST OF CASE STUDIES

LIST OF FIGURES AND TABLES

ACKNOWLEDGEMENTS

We would very much like to thank the authors of this report for the time they have spent researching the theme of HR and technology for the CIPD.

We would also like to thank the organisations that gave up their time and resources to contribute as case studies in this report:

BOC Gases

British Sky Broadcasting

Cancer Research UK

Crown Prosecution Service

IBM UK

Marks & Spencer

NHS

Norwich Union

Nortel

Transport for London

We would also like to thank the members of the project's steering group for their contributions:

Steve Foster	Northgate
Peter Hornsby	QinetiQ
Andrea Lawson	Norwich Union
Kath Lowey	Xchanging
Graeme Martin	University of Glasgow
Sally Mason	Compass
David Peters	General Motors
Martin Reddington	Martin Reddington Associates
Steve Riley	Convergys
Graham White	Surrey County Council

FOREWORD

In the last two years the CIPD has published reports on HR outsourcing, on human capital measuring and reporting and on e-learning. A common theme in these projects has been the application of technology in the process of human resource management and development – and its potential to enhance HR's contribution to the business.

This recognition led us to commission a piece of research taking a holistic look at the area of HR and technology. Issues for consideration included:

- how to improve people management – for example, by empowering line managers by making available statistics relating to absence and turnover figures
- how to unlock the benefits of technology to aid better engagement and communication with employees
- how to improve the effectiveness of the HR function – for example, by creating slick processes and readily available data so that HR can contribute more strategically.

Yet there often appears to be a problem in realising these potential benefits – for example, with the the failure of some major IT projects, comparatively slow take-up of shared services and employee and manager self-service and dissatisfaction among the users of the system.

The focus of this research has been on the impact of technology in human resource management and in particular to examine comprehensively its role in:

- the efficient delivery and support of HR activity and processes
- employee communication and engagement, and
- the resulting impact on the changing roles and skills of HR and other managers.

The first output from the research project by Cranfield School of Management is *HR and Technology: Beyond delivery* (CIPD, 2006) which provides a review of the relevant literature and draws on interviews with a number of experts on this topic.

This report is the final output and is largely based on a series of interviews with a range of stakeholders in ten case-study organisations. It aims to provide some practical advice for organisations at different stages of sophistication in their use of HR and technology. We hope you find it useful, and would welcome your feedback.

Vanessa Robinson
Rebecca Clake
Martyn Sloman
CIPD Research Advisers

EXECUTIVE SUMMARY

This report summarises the key findings from a one-year research project undertaken by the Chartered Institute of Personnel and Development on 'HR and technology'. The report focuses on the impact of technology on the HR function and on other people managers, and draws on ten case studies of organisations from a range of industry sectors.

The three central themes to this report are the impact of technology in HR on:

- the efficient delivery of HRM activity and processes
- employee engagement and communication
- the changing roles and skills of HR and other managers.

The report identifies a number of effects of technology on HRM and a number of issues on the development and implementation of information technology systems within HRM. These issues include:

- the need for a convincing business case
- the consultation process in system development
- managing the relationship between HR and IT functions
- the trade-off between a 'vanilla' product and customisation
- the need for extensive testing
- the branding of the 'solution'
- how user champions or user groups communicate and engage with employees
- education and training, including ongoing support
- user feedback.

The report then goes on to analyse the impact of technology in the areas of efficient HR delivery and support, employee communication and engagement and the skill needs that have arisen as a result of the impact of technology on HR.

THE USE OF TECHNOLOGY IN HRM 1

- **The use of technology in HRM has grown considerably in recent years and there are now extensive applications across a wide range of HRM activities.**
- **The level of sophistication of technology within HRM varies according to both the process application and the stage of development of the technology.**

INTRODUCTION

The use of technology within HRM has grown considerably in recent years: a CIPD survey in 2005 showed that 77% of organisations used some form of Human Resource Information System (HRIS). Research from Cranfield School of Management (2003) found even higher levels of use, 82% of UK organisations having some form of HRIS, although the nature of these systems varied significantly. Despite the considerable growth in the use of technology within HRM, this area is still under-researched. There are few comprehensive examinations of the impact of technology on people management and development, communication, and the HR function itself. A number of questions should be addressed. How does technology facilitate the efficient delivery and support of HR activity and processes? What is the effect of HRIS on employee communication and engagement? What is the impact of technology on the changing roles and skills of HR and other managers?

THE RESEARCH

This is the final report from the 'HR and technology' study commissioned by the CIPD in 2006. The study has been conducted by the Human Resource Research Centre at Cranfield School of Management, Cranfield University, along with associates Doone Selbie and Ray Leighton. The research has also been guided by a steering group of senior practitioners, academics and consultants in the field of e-HRM, and by representatives from the CIPD.

The focus of this research has been on the impact of technology in human resource management. Given the growth in the use of technology in HRM over recent years this subject is of increasing importance within the discipline. The purpose of this study was to provide a comprehensive examination of the impact of technology on:

- the efficient delivery and support of HR activity and processes
- employee communication and engagement
- the changing roles and skills of HR and other managers.

The starting point was a review of the relevant literature and interviews with a number of experts in this topic in order to identify the current themes in the three broad areas defined above. These were pulled together in a short publication *HR and Technology: Beyond delivery* (CIPD, 2006). This is available to download from the CIPD website at www.cipd.co.uk/changeagendas.

The outcomes of this literature review and interviews were then used to form the basis of the case-study methodology and informed the analysis of this current research.

The case studies

Ten case studies were conducted in order to provide a detailed examination of the use and impact of technology in HRM as discussed above. While it was not possible to be fully representative of the employer population through ten case studies, a wide range of organisations was chosen in order to provide an examination of the use of technology in HRM in a number of different settings. The organisations were from a range of industry sectors, were at different stages in their implementation of HRIS, and were using a range of technological solutions within different parts of the HR function. A list of the case-study organisations can be found in Table 1 on page 2.

The case studies consisted of interviews with HR directors and managers, HRIT managers, HR administrators, HR specialists, line managers, employees and technical contractors. In a number of the case studies, focus groups were held with managers or

Table 1 ◆ A summary of case-study organisations

Case study	Type of organisation	Technology	No. of employees
BOC Gases	Private sector: manufacturing	HR intranet; SAP; e-recruitment system	4,000
British Sky Broadcasting	Private sector: broadcasting and digital television	'People portal' with manager and employee self-service	15,000
Cancer Research UK	Not-for-profit medical research	E-recruitment system; HRIS with potential for manager and employee self-service; spreadsheets for payment calculations	3,500
Crown Prosecution Service	Public sector (part of the Attorney-General's Office)	E-learning (the Prosecution College); HRIS with service centre and elements of self-service	8,500
IBM UK	Large multinational: technology	HRIS and intranet with manager and employee self-service; number of stand-alone tools for appraisals, workforce planning, etc; electronic communications tools	20,000
Marks & Spencer	Large retail chain	HRIS and tools for payroll, pensions, HR administration, absence management, administration of learning and development and recruitment	68,000
NHS	Public sector: health service	Comprehensive HR and payroll system, including learning management and talent management; manager and employee self-service currently being implemented across all of the NHS	1.2 million
Nortel	Large multinational: telecommunications	SAP with various modules, including manager and employee self-service and portal; intranet accessing manager tools; number of separate but integrated tools, eg recruitment, salary planning; electronic communications tools	30,000
Norwich Union	Financial services	HRIS, including manager and employee self-service	35,000
Transport for London	Public sector: transport	SAP self-service with various modules; data uploaded and downloaded from/to various other systems, including client relationship management tool, intranet e-forms, senior management pay and bonus; other stand-alone tools, eg recruitment, knowledge system of policies and procedures	20,000

employees where this was the most convenient method of gathering data.

DEFINING TECHNOLOGY IN HRM

Human Resource Information Systems (HRIS) have developed since their increased visibility in the late 1990s. At first they were largely used for administrative and data recording purposes. Now they have developed into IT supporting processes for recruitment and selection, flexible benefits, development and e-learning. Technology is now being used to support integrated call-centres, shared services and self-service environments. As technology improves, organisations can in theory use information systems to manage an increasing number of HR processes in an effective manner in order to contribute to the availability of information and knowledge. This in turn can help free up HR professionals to play a strategic role and can lead to improved competitive advantage.

For the purpose of this research, we use Tannenbaum's (1990) definition of an HRIS as any system that helps an organisation to 'acquire, store, manipulate, analyse, retrieve and distribute information about an organisation's human resources'. We also use the term 'e-HRM' to refer to the use of technology within the HR function. This technology can range from simple spreadsheets enabling complex calculations to be performed easily, to

Figure 1 HR capability model

Source: *the National Grid HR Capability Framework, adapted from Reddington* et al *(2005)*

comprehensive HRIS solutions and e-learning. Technology may be used for different purposes within particular HR functions – for recruitment and selection, performance evaluation, compensation and benefits, training and development, health and safety, employee relations and legal issues and retention and work–life balance; or to manage HR and employee information across the entire employment cycle; as well as for processes such as e-learning.

Figure 1, above, taken from the National Grid Capability Framework, shows the main areas in which HR practitioners traditionally need to develop capabilities. Additionally, the HR function may also be involved in organisational development and change management. Technological systems can support all of these areas, as shown in the box below.

Aspect of HRM	Potential use of technology
People development and performance management	E-learning Online appraisal systems such as 360-degree feedback Training needs analysis Career management
Resourcing	Online recruitment and selection Induction packages HR planning and forecasting
Employee relations and communications	Intranet Staff surveys Shared services centres OD approaches Team development
HR information and accounting	Intranet Employee and manager self-service Metrics and human capital measurement
Retention and reward	Payroll Total rewards statements Employee self-service in creation of flexible rewards packages Reward modelling/pay reviews Pensions and benefits administration

Martinsons (1994) distinguished between the use of HRIS in 'unsophisticated' ways such as payroll and benefits administration, and 'sophisticated' uses in recruitment and selection, training and development, HR planning and performance appraisal. The advent of web-based technology has also allowed HR departments to extend services directly to managers and employees through the provision of self-service systems. A distinction may also be made between the use of modern technology to manage the HR function and other technology that can help drive new practices on substantive areas of HR such as recruitment or training. This depends on whether organisations are using the data produced by an HRIS strategically or whether they are just using the system to manage HR more efficiently.

Our case-study organisations demonstrate the variety of ways in which technology is used within HRM and also the different levels of sophistication of that technology. For example, Cancer Research UK has obtained great benefits from simple spreadsheet calculations, but has also introduced an e-recruitment system and is developing a more comprehensive HRIS. BOC Gases has also developed a system to manage its recruitment process from end to end, and the NHS includes an e-recruitment module as part of its Electronic Staff Record (ESR) system.

Technology may also be used in a more sophisticated manner. The General Shared Services team at BSkyB have introduced a spreadsheet system to manage and record employee relations cases and queries. This means that they can look back at the disciplinary and grievance advice that they have given in the past, therefore encouraging them to deal with cases in a consistent fashion. Cancer Research UK's e-recruitment system has allowed it to create a 'talent database' containing the details of previous applicants, that it can search for suitable candidates for any new vacancies that arise. Transport for London is analysing its HR data and using it to influence business strategy, while Nortel is using manager self-service to drive responsibility and decision-making further down the organisation and increase manager capability. The Crown Prosecution Service, on the other hand, initially focused its investment on e-learning, where there was a strong strategic need, showing that an organisation may use technology to manage different process areas but with a strategic purpose. Indeed, recent CIPD survey research supports this by noting the proportion of organisations that use an HRIS for a number of HR functions (see Table 2).

Most of the systems above were stand-alone rather than integrated with organisation-wide systems, so that the potential benefits of information-sharing were lost due to lack of integration.

The CIPD survey also showed that organisations commonly use technology in the form of an intranet or staff portal. This can be defined as a system where

> *computer terminals are linked so that they can share information within an organisation or within part of an organisation.*
>
> CIPD, 2005

However, this definition can be extended to

> *a tool or platform by which internal two-way communication including employee or manager self-service can be facilitated.*
>
> Emma Parry, CIPD HR Software Show, 2006

Table 2 ◆ Organisations' use of their HRIS

Function	Percentage of organisations
Absence management	85
Training and development	75
Rewards	75
Managing diversity	57
Recruitment and selection	51
Other (usually payroll)	50
Appraisal/performance management	47
HR planning	29
Knowledge management	25
Expenses	19
HR strategy	18
Communication	18

Source: *CIPD People Management and Technology Survey, 2005*

The CIPD survey showed that 71% of organisations possessed an intranet system and that these were most commonly used to provide HR information and as a facility for staff to download HR forms (see Table 3).

Table 3 ◆ Use of corporate intranet systems

Purpose	Percentage of respondents
To provide access to HR information	98
To provide a facility for downloading forms	88
To provide a facility for staff feedback	48

Source: *CIPD People Management and Technology Survey, 2005*

Most of the organisations studied provide information for employees through an intranet, including policies and practices and HR forms, although the functionality, look and indexing of these systems may differ considerably.

One of the fastest-growing trends in the delivery of HR information is 'employee self-service' (ESS): 80% of large US companies delivered some information to employees via an ESS system by 2000 (Gueutal, 2003). The CIPD *People Management and Technology* Survey in 2005 showed that 22% of UK organisations had an ESS system. These applications can give employees the ability to access and maintain HR information about themselves via the web. Some ESS systems, in organisations such as Nationwide, even allow the employee to select his or her own benefits package within the total value of the job. Likewise, manager self-service provides a variety of HR tools and information for managers. These systems can provide managers with access to information about their subordinates and give them the opportunity to analyse information in order to improve managerial effectiveness – for example, through pay modelling at salary review time or contractor tracking.

Organisations such as Nortel, BSkyB, TfL, IBM and Norwich Union have developed self-service systems for managers and employees including tools for absence management (BSkyB, Nortel, TfL, and Norwich Union), performance development (IBM, Nortel) and online payslips (Norwich Union, TfL). A number of the other case-study organisations including the NHS and Cancer Research UK have not yet implemented self-service functionality but are in the process of developing such systems.

An analysis of the use of technology within one of our case studies demonstrates how the use of technology may differ within a single organisation.

CASE STUDY 1a

THE USE OF HR TECHNOLOGY IN BOC GASES

BOC Gases is a large manufacturer of industrial gases that is divided into three lines of business – process gas solutions, industrial and special products, and BOC Edwards – and has a specialist logistics business, Gist. It employs over 30,000 people who work in 50 countries. The group has recently merged with Linde.

BOC Gases has used an SAP HR system since 1999. This system holds HR data and allows managers to access this data. The employee information contained in the system includes cost centre, job role, pay and benefits, absence and leave. SAP also stores the organisational tree and personnel actions such as salary changes and departmental moves as a piece of history. Managers access this system via the line manager desktop. They are responsible for recording absence and for entering bonus ratings on a quarterly basis and salary review details annually. One part of the business also uses the system to record hours under the annualised hours system. The system drives the payroll process (although an! SAP payroll system is not used) through a monthly report that interfaces with the payroll system. The reward team use the SAP system to produce reports.

BOC Gases introduced an e-recruitment system in 2003 in order to increase the visibility of its spend on recruitment and to improve the efficiency of the recruitment process. There is a recruitment database that sits centrally and is connected to a number of different career centres that each has a different URL. Each career centre also has its own behind-the-scenes processing and application form. The system has different levels of access for vendors, managers, administrators and HR recruiters. Managers or resourcing staff can create vacancies in the system and a corresponding advertisement. This goes through an approval process and is then posted on the corporate website, intranet, and on a number of external jobs boards. Applicants complete a form online, which is then saved to the database. It is also possible to add multiple-choice questions on which the applicant will be screened automatically. Managers can then log in to look at the applications. The system sends out automated acknowledgements and will generate rejection letters once the manager or recruiter has affirmed that a candidate has been rejected. This can be done in batches rather than individually. A summary of candidates can be viewed on screen and reports can be produced as Excel files or as a printout.

The HR intranet has recently been re-launched; the previous system was out of date and difficult to navigate. The site is accessed via the intranet home page and contains HR information, forms, news and tools such as 360-degree feedback. All of the HR policy and procedure information is now on this site and is current. The system can be navigated using menus or search functionality and is aimed primarily at the HR team but is also used by managers and employees with different levels of access.

A second case study shows how another organisation also uses SAP but for broader manager and employee self-service applications.

CASE STUDY 1b

THE USE OF HR TECHNOLOGY IN TRANSPORT FOR LONDON

Transport for London (TfL) was created in 2000 as the integrated body responsible for London's transport system including the London Buses and Underground, the Docklands Light Railway and London River Services. In addition, it manages the central London Congestion Charging scheme, the 360-mile (580-kilometre) network of main roads and all the 4,600 traffic lights. There are three operating businesses and four corporate service groups, HR being one, with about 20,000 employees in total. Each operating business has its own HR director and team of business partners and Group HR has the core HR teams which either set strategy or work across all the businesses. These include employee relations, compensation and benefits and HR Services.

TfL was formed from a number of public sector departments, which, when it came together had multiple core databases and stand-alone systems. An SAP ERP (enterprise resource planning) project covering finance, procurement and HR, introduced employee and manager self-service tools across the organisation and enabled many systems to be retired and data to be consolidated onto this one SAP system. The HR SAP project was the last part of the ERP project and occurred in late 2003. This was followed by the setting up of HR Services (a shared service centre) in 2005. The SAP system also runs the payrolls.

Over 40% of the population can access the intranet, and through this portal they can reach the SAP self-service modules and also e-forms which act as triggers for the HR Service Advisers to open cases. Anyone else who needs access to the intranet and e-forms uses a local administrator nominated specifically for this role. These cases are tracked using a CRM (client relationship management) tool that is populated with employee data so that the Advisers can identify those they are speaking with and can see the case history. The CRM tool also breaks down a case into the key tasks required to complete the case and tracks whether they are closed within the appropriate service level agreement (SLA) period. The HR Service Advisers also have access to a knowledge system storing all the company policies and procedures that they use to advise their callers at the first point of contact. Almost 90% of all calls are resolved at first point of contact by HR Services.

Managers use the e-form process to initiate actions in the SAP system, such as the creation of positions and reporting sickness as well as directly approving employee leave application. In addition, they conduct various procurement and budgeting activities. The employee self-service modules allow people to maintain their personal details, view payslips and manage their travel and expenses.

There is a separate senior manager pay and bonus system, involving a sophisticated Excel spreadsheet that enables salary and bonus planning and approval, based on a number of factors, which can then be uploaded into the SAP system avoiding duplication of data entries. In addition, there is a recruitment tool that assists in the management of job applications and the organising of assessments for applicants.

A central information management team runs both standard and specialised reports for the HR community as well as producing regular management statistics for the manager scorecard.

The type and sophistication of the technical system used within the HR function will have an effect on both the implementation of the solution and on the HR function and the wider organisation. In addition, the nature of the organisation itself will have an impact, so there are no 'right' or 'wrong' solutions. The successful implementation of an HRIS is about understanding your own organisation, highlighting key issues that you want addressed and selecting the right set of tools to do that. However, there are a number of common themes and lessons that can be drawn from the case studies, and these are discussed in the remainder of this report.

SUMMARY

The use of technology within HRM is growing rapidly and expanding to become more sophisticated and to cover a wider range of HR activities. The purpose of this study is to provide a comprehensive examination of the use and impact of information technology in HRM when considering HR activity and processes, employee engagement and communication, and the changing roles and skills of HR and other managers. Subsequent chapters examine these areas, drawing on the information collected from the case studies and the literature.

- Chapter 2 describes those lessons learned from the case studies in terms of the planning of information systems in the HR function. Particular attention is paid to the business case and the consultation and development process.
- Chapter 3 focuses on the issue of involving employees with the technology, through examples of change management, training and education.
- Chapter 4 examines the first of the three main themes of this research: the impact of the technology on the efficient delivery and support of HR activity and processes. This chapter also comments on the evaluation of this impact and upon obstacles to achieving potential efficiency savings.
- Chapter 5 looks at both the positive and negative impact of technology on employee communication and engagement – the second of the three main areas of focus.
- Chapter 6 investigates the impact of technology on the HR role and the skills of HR practitioners within the case-study organisations (the third of the three areas). It asks whether technology can enable HR practitioners to move towards becoming business partners. This chapter also looks at the impact of technology in HRM for line managers.
- Chapter 7 summarises the findings of this research and the implications for HR practice.

PLANNING FOR AN E-HRM SYSTEM 2

- **Organisations need to establish a sound business case for the introduction of technology, including a business reason for its implementation.**
- **The design of any e-HRM system should be based upon large-scale consultation with potential end-users, and on a thorough examination of existing processes.**
- **The system should be tested extensively by end-users.**
- **The branding of the system must be aligned with the employer and company brand.**

INTRODUCTION

This chapter discusses the process of developing an e-HRM system. By 'e-HRM' we mean any technological system that is used within the HR function. By 'HRIS' we mean a system that helps an organisation to 'acquire, store, manipulate, analyse, retrieve and distribute information about an organisation's human resources'. The development of any information technology system is a complex process and should be undertaken with great care and attention to detail. As we will see in this chapter, it is essential that sufficient time is allocated to the design, building and testing of an e-HRM system if that system is to have the desired impact upon HR processes. In one of our case studies, an HR manager commented:

> *It's always bigger than you think. You think you're ready, but you're not.*
>
> HR manager, University Hospital, Birmingham

The development and implementation of an HRIS should follow a structured process, as detailed in Figure 2 below.

Figure 2 The process of developing an HRIS

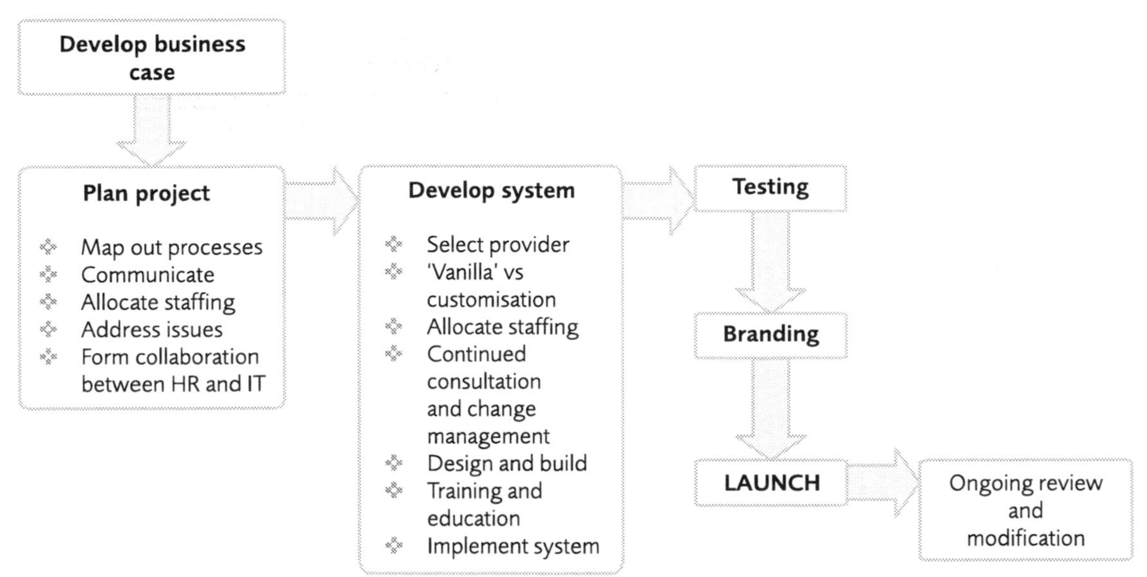

Table 4 ❖ Potential benefits for e-HR

'Hard' benefits	'Soft' benefits
❖ Reducing service delivery costs by automating key HR business processes	❖ Allowing instant processing of information – leading to reduction in cycle times
❖ Reducing correction costs by improving the accuracy of HR information	❖ Increasing employee satisfaction by improving quality of HR service and providing access to information
❖ Eliminating costs of printing and distributing information to employees by making the information available online	❖ Allowing the HR function to become a strategic partner to the business as routine administrative work is minimised
❖ Improving employee productivity by providing universal access on a 24/7 basis	❖ Potentially signalling a change towards an organisational culture that promotes initiative, self-reliance and improved internal service standards
❖ Reducing data entry and search costs through employee and manager self-service	
❖ Enabling more cost-effective decision-making through improved analysis of HR information	
❖ Minimising IT infrastructure by moving to a common HR service platform	

Source: Ministry of Manpower, Singapore (2003)

Table 5 ❖ Reasons for introducing an HRIS

Reason	Percentage of respondents
Improving quality of information available	91
Reducing administrative burden on the HR department	83
Improving speed at which information is available to the organisation	81
Improving flexibility of information to support business planning	59
Improving services to employees	56
Producing HR metrics/measures for performance management	55
Aiding human capital reporting	42
Improving productivity	39
Reducing operational costs	35
Managing peoples' working time more effectively	26
Enabling employees to access HR information	25
Facilitating the achievement of external standards	19
Improving profitability	16
Reducing headcount	8
Complying with supply-chain partner requirements	5

Source: CIPD People Management and Technology Survey, 2005

THE BUSINESS CASE

Putting together a business case for the introduction of technology in HRM may be problematic compared to technology introduction in other parts of a company. The use of an e-HRM system may not have direct financial implications in the same way that, for example, the automation of a production line may have. However, there is still a need for organisations to examine the potential benefits of using such a system so that they may justify its introduction, initially to senior management and those responsible for backing the process financially, and then to the organisation as a whole, in particular the end-users.

Research from the Singapore Ministry of Manpower (2003) divides the potential benefits of e-HR into 'hard' and 'soft' benefits (see Table 4 opposite).

The 2005 CIPD survey, *People management and technology* has also examined the reasons behind organisations' introduction of an HRIS (see Table 5, opposite) and noted that the five most popular reasons had not changed since the previous year.

Kettley and O'Reilly in their report for the Institute of Employment Studies (2003) have divided the drivers for the introduction of technology into three areas – operational drivers, relational drivers and transformational drivers.

'Operational efficiency' includes, for example, reducing overhead costs, enhancing the accuracy of data, eliminating the costs of printing and disseminating information; 'relational impact' is about changing the nature of the relationship between HRM, line managers and employees; and 'transformational impact' is about changing the HR function's role into that of a strategic business partner.

If we examine the business case put forward by one of our case-study organisations, Norwich Union, we can see that the elements of this case can be divided into these three areas (see box below). We can also see that several of the reasons cited in the CIPD survey and Ministry of Manpower report are included in this business case.

CASE STUDY 2

THE BUSINESS CASE AT NORWICH UNION

Norwich Union is the largest insurer in the UK and is part of Aviva, the world's sixth-largest insurance group, which has £291 billion of assets under management. Aviva has 60,000 employees serving 30 million customers worldwide. Norwich Union was founded in Norwich over 200 years ago but has been part of the Aviva Insurance Group since the merger of Norwich Union and CGU in 2000. Norwich Union HR consists of Business Partners, Centres of Excellence and HR Customer Services. HR Customer Services comprises HR learning and development services, HR change and communication, HR systems, MI and planning, and HR systems, which includes payroll and administration, telephone advice, recruitment and relocation services.

The company uses an Oracle HR information system with an extensive system of manager self-service. Managers can use the system to carry out fundamental changes with regard to their employees. These include salary changes, cost centre and allowances changes, processing leavers, updating and reporting absence, processing overtime payments and comparing salaries and performance ratings. The company also uses a degree of employee self-service so that employees are able to maintain personal details online, look at their payslips, request holidays, record absence, change bank account details, maintain their emergency contact and look at the above information plus performance ratings, salary, history, etc.

Norwich Union set out the drivers for their roll-out of Oracle self-service functionality in some detail. These were:

1 *Enabling line management*

Promoting a cultural shift whereby managers are enabled to take responsibility for managing their people through being able to access and maintain records.

Building the functionality to cope with a flexible workforce.

2 *Improving and simplifying core processes*

Getting the basics right by providing real-time updates and immediate access for managers.

Removing duplication of administration by enabling data entry at source.

Improving the integrity of HR data.

Providing timely and accurate information enabling more effective and proactive management of people.

Increasing online processing in order to drive the business towards standardisation and economies of scale.

3 *Adding value through HR expertise*

Removing data processing activity from HR without adding burdens on managers.

Supporting e-enablement of the business.

Allowing HR resource to move from transactional to performance-enhancing activity.

Facilitating the introduction of new HR activities online such as competencies and flexible benefits.

Encouraging individuals to take increased ownership of their own details and career management.

4 *E-enablement of HR*

Building the platform for tomorrow, today, in order to provide a progressive transactional HR system.

Maximising the use of the platform to improve administrative processes.

E-enablement of HR mirrors business practice and would be expected for a company of this size and status.

series of 100 interviews with employees to establish the requirements of such a system. Eleven requirements were identified and (following a tendering process) a system was eventually selected that satisfied those needs.

Prior to the design of ESR, the NHS held around 14 workshops in respect of each process that included users from a number of NHS Trusts. The NHS also appointed a 'process champion' for each process. These individuals were experts in their process and were responsible for deciding on the final design of their process if the participants in the workshop could not agree.

It is important that the consultation and process mapping should include all parts of the business. In one of the case-study organisations, the examination of processes neglected one part of the business. This led to difficulties in that the technology used did not fit well with the processes in this area. In addition, employees in this part of the business were somewhat resistant to the technology because they felt that they had not been properly consulted. A consultation of the type above may therefore prove invaluable in providing a system that satisfies user needs across the business, and may also help to achieve the buy-in of stakeholders to the HRIS chosen.

Collaboration between the IT and HR departments

Another issue illustrated by BSkyB is the need for effective collaboration between the HR and IT teams. This is essential if the requirements for the system are to be communicated effectively to those who are responsible for building it. BSkyB is not the only one of the companies examined to have appointed an individual to bridge the gap between HR and IT. The development and implementation of Norwich Union's HRIS was managed by an HRIT manager, and the production of ESR in the NHS has arisen from a close working relationship between IT contractors McKesson and the NHS staff. The senior management team from McKesson and the NHS project staff met on a daily basis to discuss progress and produce regular reports. Nortel has had an HRIS team for over 10 years who effectively manage the relationship between both the HR and IT communities. They work closely with their HR client, usually by process area, to ensure that any business requirements are clearly understood and that the systems are developed to meet them. They will also help in building the business cases and the budgeting process for new systems and additional SAP modules.

'The establishment of a means to manage the relationship between the HR and IT functions is something that may easily be overlooked... Yet it is fundamental...'

The establishment of a means to manage the relationship between the HR and IT functions is something that may easily be overlooked in the design and implementation of a new IT system. Yet it is fundamental to its success because a failure to establish effective communication channels between HR and IT can lead to delays and difficulties in developing the HRIS.

Customisation

The case-study information from BSkyB also suggests some conflict between the need to maintain a 'vanilla' (ie common, plain) system to enable future upgrades and the need to customise the system in order to satisfy the requirements of the business. This was recognised by the HR Technology manager as being a 'trade-off'. It is highly unlikely that a system will not require any customisation at all.

Customisation is what happens when the actual code of the 'off-the-shelf' IT system is changed, and extensive customisation may make future upgrades problematic and expensive, so it is important to allow only those customisations that are absolutely necessary.

The Nortel case study refers to its initial SAP implementation in the 1990s when the goal was to implement a 'vanilla' system with customisations only where legislative needs demanded. Considerable process standardisation took place to meet this objective. However, the roll-out and development approach was regional rather than global, and this resulted in regional concerns influencing the design, causing problems later. When the Phase 2 SAP project was launched in 2005, there was further process rationalisation work necessary to remove the earlier customisations and reach a more vanilla system. Even so, there were still some conscious decisions taken that resulted in effecting some customisations to help the manager follow through a more 'Nortel' process.

This global/regional conflict has also been highlighted in the CIPD's *International recruitment, selection and assessment* report (Sparrow, 2006) which emphasises that technology is allowing the balance to tip more towards central, common solutions.

Testing

Most of the case-study organisations appear to have undergone an extensive testing process in the same way as BSkyB. Norwich Union set up a managers' working group which was responsible for testing the functionality of the system prior to the actual roll-out. Testing is essential in order to discover any major problems with the system before it goes live, so it is important to allow sufficient time and resources for it. Testing should therefore be seen as a key stage of the development process. It is also important to have in place processes to allow evaluation and modification of a system to continue once a system is live. The NHS initially rolled out ESR in a number of pilot sites in order to facilitate this process.

Branding

It is important for a company both as an organisation and as an employer that the look and feel of the product should fit into the company's brand. The brand of an HR portal will ultimately be equated with the brand of the HR function, so it is vital to get it right. BSkyB has paid considerable attention to the brand of both the 'People Portal' and HR department through the use of its 'space-hopper' design. That this is a distinctive brand that is easily recognisable is evident in Figure 3, opposite. This design was selected to specifically reflect the values of the organisation and therefore fits well with the branding of the organisation both generally and as an employer.

Figure 3 ✧ The 'People Portal' at BSkyB – an example of branding

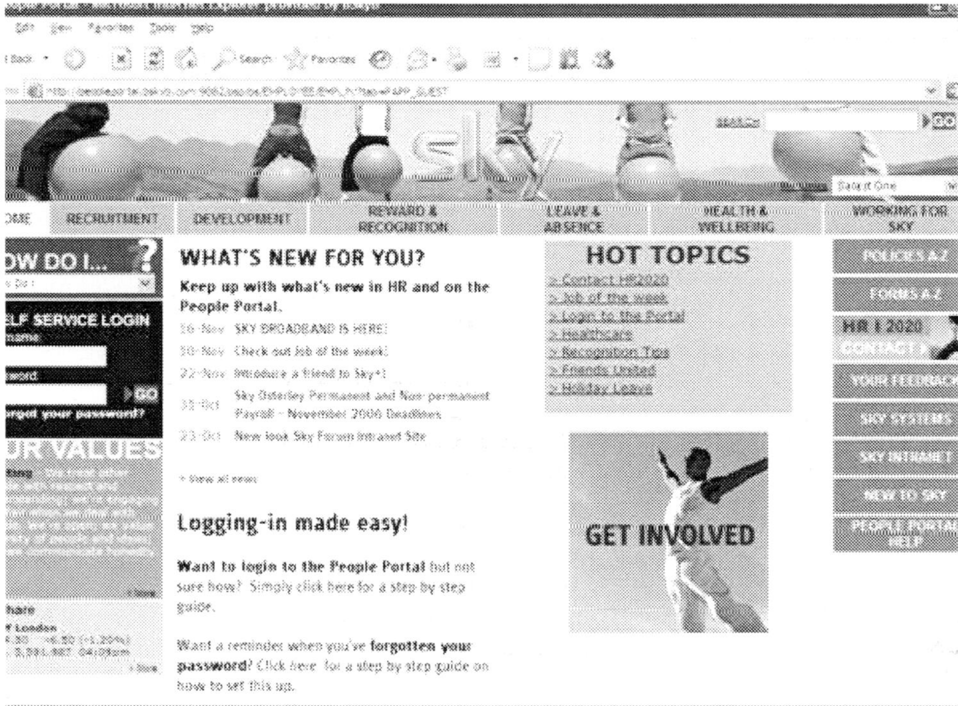

LEARNING POINTS

- Consult with as many relevant stakeholders (including subject matter experts) as possible in order to ensure that everybody's requirements are met.
- Carry out this consultation as early as possible in the process.
- Appoint 'competent and dedicated' people to take responsibility for this consultation and assign process owners to take responsibility for each process.
- Map out or examine processes thoroughly.
- Create a strategy for managing the relationship between the HR team and both internal and external IT people.
- Be aware of the trade-off between using a vanilla process and necessary customisation. Some customisation is inevitable, but stick to that which is absolutely necessary.
- Make sure you test the system sufficiently to identify any problems before the system is live.
- Consider the brand of the organisation and HR department in the design of the technology.

SUMMARY

This chapter has considered a number of factors on the design and development of an information system in HR. First, consideration was given to the nature of the business case for technology in HR in terms of the possible components of that case and the need to identify a business driver and to align the business case with the IT and business strategy as well as the HR strategy. Second, issues were examined surrounding the development of technological systems and the importance of extensive consultation with stakeholders and the management of the relationship between the HR team and IT team was highlighted. In addition, there was a discussion of the need to consider the degree of customisation of the product, the testing of the system, and branding.

This is not an exhaustive list of those factors that should be considered when designing an HRIS. They are useful suggestions to avoid potential problems within the process, based upon the case-study organisations. Chapter 3 focuses on an area of importance in the successful implementation of technology – that of engaging the potential users of a system.

OBTAINING STAKEHOLDER BUY-IN 3

- **The process of involving employees should be started as early as possible in the design and implementation process in order to ensure the buy-in of employees.**
- **This can be achieved through the use of sponsors or champions of the system.**
- **The need for education and training of users should not be underestimated, and such programmes should be designed carefully.**
- **Ongoing feedback mechanisms for users are important in order to maintain user engagement, understanding and interest.**

INTRODUCTION

The success of any technological system, in HR or otherwise, is dependent on the acceptance of its users. No system will become fully embedded within an organisation if potential users – the HR team, managers and employees – do not fully buy in to its adoption. It is therefore essential that steps are taken to ensure the engagement of potential users with any technological system within HRM.

The introduction of an HRIS should be managed in the same way as any other organisational change, those involved being communicated with, educated and consulted throughout the implementation process. For more information on how to effectively manage a change process, see CIPD's *HR's Role in Organising: Shaping change* (Whittington and Molloy, 2005).

This process should be started as early as possible, an effort being made to help users understand the rationale and business case behind the new system and to enable users to be a part of the design and implementation process.

In the last chapter it was suggested that stakeholders should be consulted throughout the development of the system, from the identification of user requirements to testing or piloting the system, to providing ongoing feedback once the system is live. Further steps that may be taken in order to involve potential users are best understood through an examination of our case studies.

CASE STUDY 4

THE ENGAGEMENT OF USERS IN THE NHS

The National Health Service is the public sector provider of health care in the UK and is managed by the Department of Health. It was set up in 1948 and is now the largest organisation in Europe, with a 2006-7 budget of £96 billion. The NHS is also the largest employer in Europe, with well over a million employees, and is divided into 302 Primary Care Trusts, 290 Hospital Trusts, 13 Ambulance Trusts and a small number of Care Trusts and Mental Health Trusts (over 600 Trusts in total). The NHS is managed locally by an HR team, usually one in each Trust. This has meant that there is generally no consistency between HR processes between Trusts.

The NHS is in the process of implementing the Electronic Staff Record (ESR), a national fully-integrated HR and payroll system that will be used by all 600+ NHS organisations by the end of 2008. In addition to core HR and payroll modules, ESR includes recruitment, learning management, absence, talent management, and employee and manager self-service. The system is currently used only by the HR teams in each Trust, but will eventually be used by managers and employees as well. The self-service functionality will allow employees to view and maintain their personnel records, view past payslips, update competencies and qualifications, enrol on training courses and participate in online development reviews. In addition, managers will be able to approve changes made by employees, record contractual changes and data on the transfer, promotion or termination of employees and to conduct online development reviews.

The involvement of users is of paramount importance within the NHS due to the sheer scale of the implementation of ESR. At the time of the case study, ESR core functionality was live in 274 Trusts (505,000 staff). The system will be launched in around 50 hospitals (100,000 staff) every two months. In addition to the scale of the implementation, user acceptance has been problematic due to the amount of cynicism about change that exists within the Service, particularly technological change, and the fact that this is a national implementation whereas the Trusts are traditionally managed locally. It has therefore been essential that the NHS should approach the involvement of its employees with the technology in a strategic manner.

User involvement in the NHS has been approached using a number of methods. The project team has tested what they are doing with users and obtained feedback throughout the process. A senior user and project board has been appointed in order to ensure that decisions are made in the interests of users. This board is also responsible for obtaining feedback from the user and for providing information to the user. The role of the senior user is also to act as an ambassador for the system and to be a point of contact for users.

An interim user group was established throughout the pilot process, including the leads from each pilot site. This group helped to refine the solution, identify problems and test views. As the number of NHS Trusts using ESR has increased, it has become impractical to continue with a single user group, so a network of user groups has been established. There is now a user group in each Strategic Health Authority and a national user group that consists of two members from each regional group. The regional groups plan their agendas around the agenda of the national group so that they can feed information into the national group. At each meeting, three critical issues for solution are identified and then fed into the enhancement process to be addressed. The groups have created a critical issues log so that the issues can be tracked, showing what has been done about each. The project board is also putting together a 'lessons learned' brochure and is devising a series of seminars so that users can see what they have learned as they have moved through the implementation process.

User acceptance depends on the change management processes that have been undertaken by each individual Trust. Communication is mainly the responsibility of the HR team within that Trust. The fact that Trusts are managed independently and have different existing HR systems makes central change management procedures difficult. The introduction of the system is a massive culture change for some Trusts because the new system may be very different from the system being used before. It is therefore important that the champions of the system in each Trust create a 'vision' for its use and impact. A super-user is appointed in each Trust to look at how the implementation will impact on processes. The super-users receive more training than other users and are trained at an earlier stage in the implementation. It is their job to act as the ambassadors for ESR within their Trust. The super-users also act as a point of contact for people with problems in using the system. It is their job to log a support call with the IT contractor if required.

The training for users of ESR was designed centrally via consultation with users. Interviews with core users were held in order to establish the preferred style of training so that a suitable approach to the training could be taken. The interviews showed that users wanted classroom-style training, so training was designed on this basis. Issues later arose in respect of users travelling to training sessions, so a blended approach was adopted including an element of e-learning. The e-learning uses a 'try me, guide me' approach whereby users are guided through the system first and then are allowed to try each process and are given feedback. It was seen as important to allow the users to try the system in a safe environment where they could make mistakes without risk. A user manual was also produced. There is some debate among users over whether the training provided was adequate. There was also some feeling that the number of people who would require training had been underestimated, at least in the early waves of the implementation.

Those users of ESR who were interviewed seemed to be well engaged with the technology, at least in terms of appreciating the rationale behind its introduction. Those involved in the training of users appear to have gone to great lengths to emphasise the importance of consistent HR processes within the NHS, and this has meant that many users have bought into this idea. There is still a degree of cynicism among some users as to whether ESR will ultimately be successful, but this may be eroded over time. The project board has recently drafted a second-stage communications strategy and members are frequently speaking at conferences in order to overcome any remaining cynicism. A number of Trusts are now planning the implementation of the manager and employee self-service modules of ESR. A project has been established to examine the benefits of these additional modules, involving the HR teams from a number of Trusts. It remains to be seen how well managers and employees will engage with the rationale and practicalities of the technology should self-service be introduced.

A number of issues can be drawn out from the experience of the NHS and our other case studies.

COMMUNICATION WITH USERS

It is vital that potential users of any system should receive communications at every step of the development and implementation process. They should be informed of the reasons behind a system's introduction and regularly updated on progress so that they are made to feel part of the process. It is important that an organisation constructs a clear communications plan at the outset of any implementation. The exact nature of this plan will depend on who the technology affects, because all of these individuals should be included in the communication process.

In the case of Nortel, monthly webcasts to the HR and IT communities were started around seven months before the manager and employee self-service SAP tool went live. This was then extended to a programme of HR and manager roadshows across the key cities with the highest employee populations showing example scenarios within the system to help illustrate the new workflow processes.

Prior to the introduction of ESR in the NHS, representatives of the project team participated in several service events in order to ensure that potential users were aware of the forthcoming changes. BSkyB used a number of communications strategies, including promoting the new 'People Portal' by projecting the home page onto the wall in the staff canteen. The company also produced a number of articles in its internal publications and on the intranet. Once the portal had been launched, the HR team held a competition in which employees were asked to find pieces of information on the portal in order to win a prize. The prize for winning the competition was a space-hopper (which as the logo of the portal fits in with the brand of the portal). BOC Gases also had an extensive communications programme when it re-launched its HR portal. This included the use of email, the company intranet, announcements, articles in BOC Gases publications and cascade briefings.

The importance of communication in the implementation of technology cannot be emphasised enough. It is impossible for users to engage with a system of which they are unaware. Norwich Union has found that awareness of the full functionality of its HRIS is still relatively low among employees, despite the fact that 98% of employees are now using the system. Employees are often unsure of the system's functionality and blame this on the fact that updates to the system have not been publicised widely. Within the CPS, e-learning was introduced incrementally so that lawyers who prefer a verbal culture have slowly shifted their learning style to incorporate e-learning. The positive experiences of e-learning in the CPS have encouraged the Department to move towards more self-service and a greater strategic role based on data from the HRIS.

Employees should be informed about the system from as early as possible using as many channels as possible, throughout the implementation. They should also be encouraged to use the system, if necessary by removing alternative means of conducting a particular process. For instance, Norwich Union is in the process of removing paper payslips so that employees are forced to go online to obtain details of their pay, while TfL publish the payslips online three to four days before the paper payslips are distributed, thus encouraging employees to look online to get the information – in fact, many employees have already opted only to receive the information online.

SPONSORS AND USER GROUPS

One of the steps that the NHS has taken is to appoint 'champions' of the system, these being a senior user for the service and a 'super-user' in each Trust. This method provides a means of communication with users, both by providing users with information and by obtaining feedback from the users. These individuals also promote the system, therefore encouraging the support of other users. Setting up effective channels of communication is important in the process of engaging users with the system because it makes people feel involved in the implementation and development process. The NHS has also achieved this through the use of regional and national user groups. Norwich Union used a similar process in the development of its HRIS by getting a business manager focus group to provide feedback. Norwich Union has also set up a working group whose responsibility is to obtain 100% registration on the system (for those who have access), to actively promote the system and to continuously improve the system based on user feedback.

> 'Setting up effective channels of communication is important in the process of engaging users with the system because it makes people feel involved...'

The open support of senior management may also help to engage employees with the system. Having a member of senior management to 'sponsor' the implementation by promoting it within the organisation may also encourage managers and employees to buy in to using the technology.

In Nortel, the CEO was a key sponsor for the introduction of manager and employee self-service and visibly supported the development and introduction of the SAP system as a tool to deliver the Business and HR Evolution programmes. He explained his vision in a video that was shown at all the roadshows during which a local business leader also promoted the project by championing its reasons, discussing impacts and answering questions from the audience. An HR leader facilitated these roadshows and explained the HR Evolution programme, but the project was promoted as a business project, not just an HR project. This visible support from the senior management for the project and the recognition and understanding of the changing role of managers and HR helped to move the organisation forward in accepting the changes that were to come.

The TfL project team engaged well with the senior management teams and had excellent representation in the Business Improvement Processes Steering Group. The expectation was that the key messages would filter down through the management hierarchy regarding the vision and culture changes expected by the introduction of HR Services and the SAP deployment. In retrospect, although senior sponsorship was high, surveys have subsequently identified a need to get closer to the end customer. They show that adoption and use of the tools and HR Services has

IMPACT ON THE EFFICIENCY OF HR ACTIVITY AND PROCESSES 4

- **Technology can have a major positive impact on HR processes by making them faster, more efficient, cheaper, more accurate, more transparent and consistent.**
- **The measurement of these effects may be difficult but can be achieved through metrics showing costs, cycle time, accuracy or customer satisfaction.**
- **The integration of HR systems with each other and with other organisational systems and the removal of parallel systems may facilitate greater efficiency savings.**

INTRODUCTION

This chapter examines the impact of information technology in HR on the efficiency of HRM activity and processes. The business cases proposed in Chapter 2 suggested that the introduction of an HRIS may have an impact on the delivery and support of HR processes in terms of, among other things, speed, efficiency and cost. This chapter examines the *actual* impact of technology on the efficiency of HR activity and processes via further examination of our case studies. It therefore aims to answer the question:

Does the introduction of an HRIS actually provide those benefits as suggested in the business case?

Table 6 Success in meeting objectives – worldwide respondents reporting successful and somewhat successful

	North America (%)	Rest of the world (%)
Improving data accuracy	92	82
HR staff acceptance	91	100
Employee acceptance	84	88
Manager acceptance	84	82
Employee services improvement	80	88
Meeting administrative cost savings goal	77	59
Enabling HR to service the organisation more strategically	76	81
Aligning workforce with organisational objectives	70	47
Accountability	70	63
Enabling the organisation to recruit key talent	68	41
Enabling employees and managers to make better decisions	67	59
Revenue growth	42	59

Source: *CedarCrestone 2006 Workforce Technologies and Service Delivery Approaches Survey, Ninth Annual Edition*

The results of the CIPD survey *People management and technology* (CIPD, 2005) suggest that HRIS deliver slightly (but not significantly) better against *information* criteria such as improving the speed that information is available and the quality of that information, compared to *economic* criteria such as reducing headcount and operational costs and improving productivity and profitability.

The consultancy CedarCrestone, in their recent survey of 324 organisations, examined organisations' success at meeting their objectives for using technology (see Table 6 on page 23). Because the respondents to this survey were those responsible for the HRIS, the results may be more positive than is actually the case, but can still give us an impression of the relative success of technology at meeting a number of objectives. Both this research and the CIPD survey contain a number of items relating to the role of the HR function. The potential effects of technology in this area are discussed in Chapter 6; this chapter focuses on the impact of technology on the efficiency of HR activity and processes.

The first output from this research was *HR and Technology: Beyond delivery* (CIPD, 2006) which discussed the impact that technology may have on a number of HR processes, including recruitment and selection, benefits administration and training and development. We can see that the introduction of technology within the HR function may have a significant impact on the delivery of HR activity and processes. An analysis of our case-study organisations may help us to achieve a greater understanding of this impact.

CASE STUDY 5a

THE IMPACT OF TECHNOLOGY ON HR PROCESSES IN CANCER RESEARCH UK

Cancer Research UK is the world's leading independent organisation dedicated to cancer research and was formed in 2002 following the merger of The Cancer Research Campaign and the Imperial Cancer Research Fund. The organisation's objectives are to carry out world-class research, to develop effective treatments, to reduce the number of people affected by cancer, to provide authoritative information regarding cancer, and to work with the UK Government to ensure that cancer stays at the top of the health agenda. It is almost entirely funded by donations from the public and therefore conducts a large amount of fundraising through over 30,000 volunteers. The charity has a network of around 650 shops and 1,000 local fundraising groups. Cancer Research UK has approximately 3,500 paid employees, including over 3,000 doctors, scientists and nurses that are based (bar one) in the UK.

Cancer Research UK has adopted, or is in the process of adopting, three main technological systems: first, an online recruitment system; second, a number of spreadsheets to carry out complex calculations; and finally, a comprehensive HRIS that will eventually facilitate self-service HR processes.

Before the implementation of the online recruitment system, Cancer Research UK's recruitment processes were largely paper-based. A copy of each CV that had been received for a particular vacancy would be sent to the appropriate line manager for consideration, while another copy would be filed and stored by the resourcing team. This process was described by members of the resourcing team as 'slow' due to the reliance on the postal service, and also 'cumbersome' due to the need to process and store large quantities of paper. In addition, candidate details were entered into a computer database manually, which led to a number of mistakes due to human error.

These processes are now conducted entirely online and communications are conducted via email. Candidate data is entered by the candidates themselves via the online application process. This has had a number of effects on recruitment processes. First, the process is considerably faster. The previous method of loading jobs onto the recruitment website required the use of spreadsheets and support from the IT team, and would take one member of the resourcing team approximately one day a week. This was very problematic, especially in ensuring accuracy of the job details. If jobs were entered onto the system incorrectly or needed details changing, it took considerable effort and time. The new system works in 'real time', so jobs and any subsequent changes are instant. Support from the IT team is no longer necessary. Closing dates for applications can be maintained due to the speed of the communications via the online system (there is no longer any need to 'wait for the post'), applications are sent immediately to line managers, and the data is readily accessible via the recruitment portal. Second, because the candidate data is now entered directly by the candidate, there are fewer errors in the information, so making the process significantly more accurate.

The use of spreadsheets for calculating annual leave, maternity pay, redundancy entitlements and 'top-up pay' has also led to considerable improvements in speed and accuracy. The HR Operations manager described how, previously, it could take two to three hours to collect the relevant information and make the calculation, whereas the process now takes a matter of minutes. The fact that these calculations have now been standardised and automated also means that they are accurate. The HRIS is in the early stages of implementation. However, this HRIS is already having some effect on HR processes in that HR data is now readily available and can be produced easily, quickly and accurately.

Cost savings

The HR department has not yet conducted a full analysis of the impact of any of the three new systems on cost. However, the Resourcing manager explained that cost savings on the resourcing budget had already been achieved in two areas. Firstly, because candidate data no longer needed to be entered into a database manually, the headcount within the resourcing team has been reduced by one. And because the price of maintaining the online recruitment system is lower than this individual's salary and costs per annum, this represents a significant cost saving. In addition, the move from a system that used a large amount of paper to an online system has saved administration costs, although an exact figure was not available for either of these cost savings.

The use of an HRIS is also expected to lead to significant cost savings within the HR department, although the exact extent of these will not be known for some time. The payroll function has historically been outsourced to an external company. The use of the HRIS for payroll has therefore enabled the organisation to bring this back in-house, so saving those outsourcing costs. The eventual move to a self-service system may also lead to cost savings through headcount reductions.

GENERAL IMPACT

It can be seen from an examination of the use of technology within Cancer Research UK that technology may affect the delivery of HR processes in a number of ways.

Speed and efficiency

Technology is commonly used to make processes within HR faster and more efficient. This is true with regard to Cancer Research UK's e-recruitment system, as staff now no longer have to wait for the post to receive applications and communicate electronically. The use of spreadsheets for calculating a range of payments has reduced the time required for these from several hours to a few minutes.

The impact of technology on the speed and efficiency of HR activity is also apparent within the other case studies. The use of an e-recruitment system within BOC Gases has allowed the system to operate in 'real time' and for managers to review application forms directly, thus making the process considerably more efficient. The use of technology can also remove the need for information to be entered again by an HR administration team because it is directly entered into the system at source. The use of technology for processes such as appraisals and compensation planning within IBM has led to efficiency savings as managers now record information directly into the system. This is also true of salary reviews, bonus ratings and absence recording within BOC Gases and Nortel. The system within BOC Gases will also generate letters for salary reviews easily, so removing the need for HR administrators to perform this function. Within TfL all the senior management pay and bonus planning information is managed on a sophisticated Excel spreadsheet. The data is then directly uploaded into the SAP systems avoiding duplicate data entry but enabling centralised reporting.

The automation of processes and the entering of information directly by managers means that the amount of time needed for transactions is reduced considerably. It also removes the need for duplicate keying in that data is entered by the HR administration team, thus improving the efficiency of the process. The automatic processing of data and the generation of emails or letters also improves efficiency.

Accuracy

As discussed in Chapter 2, the removal of duplicate keying and the fact that data is entered at the source (eg by the manager or job applicant themselves) leads to improved levels of accuracy in the information contained in HR systems. This has proved to be a major benefit of the HRIS in Cancer Research UK, BSkyB and Norwich Union.

> **'…improvements in accuracy and efficiency may only be realised if HR processes have been examined properly during the system development process…'**

It should be noted that improvements in accuracy and efficiency may only be realised if HR processes have been examined properly during the system development process, and areas for potential improvement identified (see Chapter 2).

Transparency and consistency

One of the main benefits of the move to ESR within the NHS was the creation of consistent processes across Trusts. Previously, Trusts had managed HR processes independently and conducted HR processes in different ways, meaning that it was impossible to analyse the service as a whole or to benchmark processes across the NHS. The NHS provides an extreme example of the impact that technology can have on consistency of processes due to its size. However, the use of technology can also be beneficial in this manner within any organisation. BSkyB has now moved the consistent HR processes across the different parts of the business, thereby allowing the effective monitoring of the previously problematic area of absence. Marks & Spencer currently uses different processes in the shared services centre and store administration teams and is therefore planning to use technology as a means to move to consistent processes across the company.

The use of technology for HR processes may also make them more transparent. A line manager from BSkyB described how

> *Previously, we would submit paper forms that would be passed from person to person. These would get lost and then we would get accused of never submitting the form in the first place. The new system means that we can find where an action is in the process at any one time.*

Cost savings

The potential impact of technology on costs has already been discussed in Chapter 2 and so will not be examined again in detail here. Within Norwich Union, headcount reductions due to the introduction of self-service have led to a cost reduction of around £120,000. The move to online payslips will also lead to a further to look online first or by coaching them in how to find the information, rather than simply answering the question directly.

Also in Norwich Union, while managers have the discretion to use self-service to record holidays, the research indicated that a number of managers were still using traditional holiday charts. It is difficult to force managers to use a new system, particularly in that it may have a negative effect on engagement, but the fact that parallel systems are being used should at least be investigated and addressed. In TfL, if users have not accessed their systems over the past six weeks, their access is cut off and they have to reapply for access. This could be seen as counterproductive but it helps to identify those who are not using the system so that attention can be focused on them in an endeavour to understand what their issues are with the system and new processes.

SUMMARY

This chapter has examined the impact of technology on the efficient delivery of HR activity and processes. The use of technology can make HR processes faster and more efficient, more accurate, more consistent and transparent and cheaper. Some processes would not be possible without an e-application. The evaluation of these effects may be problematic, particularly if the introduction of technology has been combined with a change in HR structure. The impact of technology can sometimes be measured using comparisons of cycle times, accuracy or costs pre- and post-implementation or through the more subjective measure of customer satisfaction. It has also been noted that efficiency savings due to the implementation of technology in HR can be increased through the integration of the technology with other systems and through the elimination of parallel HR processes.

IMPACT ON EMPLOYEE ENGAGEMENT AND COMMUNICATION 5

- **Information technology can facilitate communication and people management, particularly within a dispersed workforce.**
- **HR information may be more readily available through the use of an HR intranet, leading to well-informed and therefore well-engaged employees.**
- **The use of technology can facilitate the use of flexible working practices such as home-working.**
- **Over-reliance on technology for communication can result in difficulties with relationship- and team-building within the organisation.**

INTRODUCTION

We have already noted the need for communication with employees in respect of the implementation of a technological system in HR. This chapter examines the impact of technology on communication and employee engagement within an organisation once it has been implemented.

Technology can be used to facilitate two-way communication between management and employees as well as between HR and the workforce. There can be downward communication from management to employees, or upward communication in the form of feedback from employees to management. Effective communication within organisations can have a significant influence on the motivation and commitment of employees. This is demonstrated in evidence from the CIPD (Guest and Conway, 2004) on the psychological contract, which finds that employee voice is one of the HR practices that contributes to commitment, motivation and loyalty to an organisation. Employees who are kept well-informed and who are made to feel that their feedback is valued by the organisation are more engaged with that organisation, affecting their attendance and performance.

The CIPD's latest employee engagement research, *Working Life: Employee attitudes and engagement* (Truss *et al*, 2006), also highlights the positive impact that flexible working and a good work–life balance can have on employee satisfaction and engagement. Technology can be an important enabler of more flexible working practices.

Technology can play an important part in ensuring effective communication. The use of electronic methods for communication and people management may have an impact on relationships within an organisation and the engagement of individuals both with each other and with the company as a whole. For example, the use of an HR intranet may change the nature of communication between line managers and the HR team, because managers will no longer contact the HR team to ask for information. The introduction of employee self-service so that employees can modify their own personal details will also have a direct impact on employees. Giving employees round-the-clock access to critical personal information, as well as the responsibility for ensuring that the information in that system is accurate and complete, may empower the workforce and allow employees to develop some ownership over this data by making them self-sufficient.

One of the aims of this research was to investigate the impact of technology in HR on employee engagement and communication. This chapter therefore examines this issue using the information from our case studies. For this purpose we focus mainly on the use of technology within IBM, because IBM uses technology extensively for communication and people management.

CASE STUDY 6

EMPLOYEE ENGAGEMENT AND COMMUNICATION IN IBM

IBM is the world's largest information technology company with total revenues of $91.1 billion in 2005 across its three major markets of IT services, hardware and software. IBM has approximately 329,000 employees in 75 countries, serving clients in 174 countries and is organised into three 'geographies' – the Americas, Europe, and Asia-Pacific. IBM UK employs approximately 20,000 employees. Human Resources is organised at three levels: global, geography (Europe), and country. There is a shared services centre (HRSC) based in Budapest, which supports approximately 100,000 employees across Europe, which is part of IBM's Business Performance Transformation Services organisation (which also undertakes HR outsourcing for other companies).

companies, because of the nature of the workforce. Indeed, the reliance on technology for communication is growing due to the global nature of many organisations.

Technology can facilitate employee engagement through the greater ease of communication, the increased availability of information and the ability to work at home. Alternatively, over-reliance on technology can also have a negative impact on employee engagement in terms of isolation and difficulties in relationship-building. These issues should be taken into account and addressed if necessary when implementing technology in HR.

IMPACT ON THE ROLE AND SKILLS OF HR AND OTHER MANAGERS 6

- **The use of technology in HR can lead to a reduction in administration and transactional work, allowing more time for value-added and strategic work.**
- **The introduction of technology can be used to facilitate a change in HR structure to a shared services and business partner model thereby requiring additional skill sets in the HR and shared services communities.**
- **The use of manager self-service functionality can lead to increased responsibility, access to and ownership of data for managers, but can also lead to increased workload.**

INTRODUCTION

Over recent years, considerable attention has been paid to the changing role of the HR function. There has always been an administrative rule-enforcement aspect to the role of HR. The use of technology may not only make HR more efficient but may also facilitate a change in emphasis for the HR function to become more strategic within the organisation.

Recent authors such as Ulrich (1997) have argued that HRM should become a strategic business partner, in addition to performing the administrative or transactional role, the 'change agent' and the 'employee champion' roles. The use of technology may facilitate this assumption of roles by automating much of the administrative work that the HR function would usually perform. Indeed, research by Watson Wyatt (2002) demonstrated that the most commonly recognised business benefit of e-HR is

> *allowing HR to re-focus on becoming a strategic business partner.*

Figure 4, below, illustrates the hierarchical roles that the HR function may play within an organisation. Many people have traditionally been involved with administrative activity (shown at the bottom of the HR value pyramid). The use of information technology replaces much of the administrative and data-gathering and analysis work required at all levels.

Figure 4 HR value pyramid

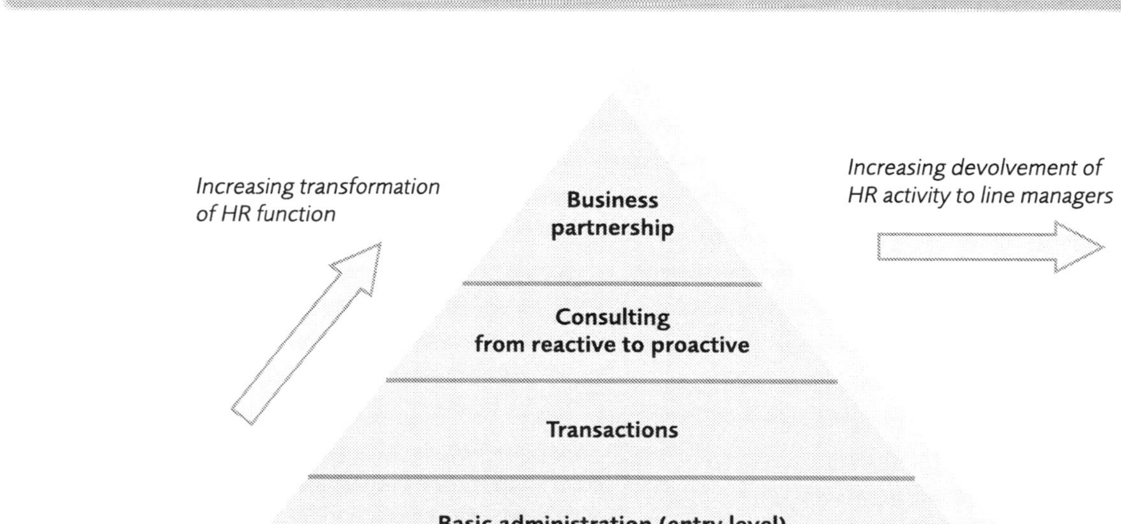

Source: adapted from Reddington et al *(2005)*

work and performance continually monitored and reviewed by their team leaders. The technology that they use can track the speed that they work at and the number of open cases, amongst other metrics. These cases would include the creation of a new position in the SAP organisation hierarchy and the generation of an employment offer following a successful interviewing process.

Often, the change in HR structure is not possible without the associated introduction of technology because it is the automation of systems and the removal of administrative workload that facilitates the creation of a shared services HR centre.

FACILITATION OF A STRATEGIC DATA-DRIVEN HR ROLE

One of the most significant outcomes of the use of technology within HR appears to be the availability of accurate and detailed information. HRIS can produce in theory a variety of reports at the touch of a button, thereby allowing HR practitioners to make data-driven decisions. But there can be practical problems in producing meaningful information in a usable format and avoiding information overload. The availability of information can also facilitate a change in the role of the HR function as it enables HR practitioners to become providers of data on which management decisions can be based and to make more strategic decision themselves based on accurate HR information. The movement of HR practitioners into this advisory or consultancy role not only requires consultancy skills but also requires a certain degree of data analysis skills so that they can read and interpret HR data effectively.

The CIPD's recent research *What's the Future for Human Capital?* (CIPD, 2006) highlights the pioneering work of the Royal Bank of Scotland in human capital evaluation. The strategy, according to Greg Aitken, Head of Employee Research and Measurement, depends on:

> *existing HR staff being trained and developed in business-facing partnering skills.*

Aitken places a premium on the system being capable of easy use by both specialists and general HR staff as well as employees and line managers. He is particularly proud of the fact that anyone using the new RBS HR toolkit need make a maximum of only four clicks of the mouse to access the information they need.

> **'...research also highlights the importance of training and the new skills needed for HR practitioners to operate effectively...'**

This research also highlights the importance of training and the new skills needed for HR practitioners to operate effectively in these strategic data-driven roles.

As mentioned earlier, the new organisation structure in Nortel has Core HR Strategy teams whose primary role is to analyse information across the company from the various HR systems and design the company's future people strategies. The HRIS within Cancer Research UK has meant that the HR team can produce statistics relating to a variety of HR processes, which can then be used as a basis for HR and managerial decision-making. For example, the system can produce reliable information on the make-up of the current workforce in respect of age, gender and ethnicity. This information may be used as a basis for an examination and review of recruitment and retention processes in order to improve the diversity of the workforce. The provision of reliable information has improved the credibility of the HR role, and this has led HR into an advisory role. It is hoped that it will eventually lead to HR's becoming a full business partner as they can give high-quality advice. HR advisers can now take information into discussions with managers and can help provide remedies to problems because they have the necessary information at hand.

A similar experience occurred in TfL. It has set up a group information management team who run regular reports and help provide data identifying trends and areas that the business needs to investigate to improve its efficiency. This team of data analysts are actually HR staff who can understand and interpret the data, and are not IT analysts. The team generate both standard reports for the monthly manager's scorecard as well as more complicated reports requested by the HR business partners. HR requests for reports are submitted via specific forms, and there is a five-day turnaround service provided by the team. There has been significant value obtained from having a centralised team with excellent understanding and knowledge of the data, because they know the right questions to ask to ensure that the correct information is extracted, and they also use consistent assumptions when running the reports.

If the information produced by an HRIS is to provide a means by which HR practitioners can become more strategic, then it is essential that it is managed properly. Cancer Research UK has created the role of 'People data manager' specifically to create HR reports. BSkyB has also appointed an HR technical analyst to look at the measures that can be pulled off the People Portal and how this information can be used within the business.

IMPACT ON LINE MANAGERS

The introduction of technology in HRM, particularly if that technology includes some manager self-service functionality, will also have an impact on line managers within the organisation. Many of the functions managers perform, such as recruitment, appraisal, training and development, have become e-enabled, as illustrated by the case of the CPS's extensive use of e-learning to enable the learning and continuing development of the 3,000 prosecutors in the UK, who use the Prosecution College. Managers may have increased access to HR information via an HR intranet, but may also be expected to take increased responsibility or ownership for data concerning their team, and may suffer a resulting increase in workload. If this change is not managed effectively, as discussed above, managers may resent the introduction of the new technology and the resulting change in their role.

CASE STUDY 7b

IMPACT ON OTHER MANAGERS WITHIN NORTEL

One of the major goals of Nortel's HR Evolution project – which included the SAP implementation – was to increase manager effectiveness and accountability in respect of the management of employees. This was achieved through a combination of increased responsibility for people management processes as well as greater empowerment to impact the business. A key change expected of managers was for their behaviour to become more open, demonstrating a willingness to take responsibility for the continuous improvement of their own skills as well as the way they approached their work challenges. The role of the people manager now involves decision-making in areas that may not have been demanded in the past. Clear objective-setting and communication of expectations, open discussion of issues that affect performance and honest feedback are all key abilities required of the manager. Although not new, an effective tool to monitor and manage these roles radically impacts on how consistently they are implemented.

The leadership team expects people managers to make decisions as if they themselves owned the business. In the past, managers experienced a certain amount of bureaucracy involving multiple levels of approval prior to executing HR transactions like a salary change, a promotion or a hiring decision. Now managers are held accountable for people changes that impact on their budgets. The manager self-service system supports a much more streamlined process of one-over-one approval. This increases the ability of managers to make decisions that directly impact on employees and the business. The objective is empowerment, to push decision-making further down the business and provide the enablers for managers to actively manage their people within the context of their business objectives, approved budgets, employee policies and laws. The HR systems help deliver the transactional processes and provide the information sources referred to above.

The manager performs this function using the SAP toolkit and the Manager's Website, as mentioned in the earlier case study 7a.

Manager self-service tools inevitably require managers to be responsible for delivering transactional tasks and understanding people-related processes that in the past would have been administered and handled by HR process experts or administrative staff. In practice, there were too many HR staff touching every part of the transactional work. Now managers are expected to enter information directly onto the SAP system rather than using a paper-based system with multiple levels of approval. They have the responsibility for ensuring that employee salaries, cost centres and location details are accurate as well as ensuring that the organisational hierarchy is correct. This automation by self-service empowers managers and raises all regions to the same level of competence at the same time, but it does result in role redefinition both for managers and HR.

We can see that the use of technology in HR may have a significant impact on the role of line managers as well as on the role of HR practitioners in two ways.

Increased responsibility, data access, ownership and workload

The example from Nortel above clearly shows that the introduction of technology, particularly manager self-service functionality, leads to an increased level of responsibility which includes the access to and ownership of data for managers. Managers may be responsible for maintaining their employees' company-related information, for recording absence and for processing salary changes. This is also true within Norwich Union in that managers have become self-sufficient. The fact that managers may now be performing administrative or transactional tasks that were previously performed by HR also means that they may experience an increase in workload. However, in Norwich Union the managers have always had to complete a form to change individual records – the difference with self-service is that they now do this online. In BSkyB, the introduction of manager self-service has merely automated many of the tasks that managers were already responsible for, and has therefore made these tasks more efficient.

The potential increase in responsibility and workload is not always received well by line managers. A number of managers within BOC Gases felt that entering salary changes, bonus ratings and absence details into SAP was not a good use of their time and should be done by the HR team. Some of the managers within IBM felt that they no longer received sufficient support from the HR department due to the move to manager self-service and a shared services HR structure. Nortel has tried to minimise this feeling by introducing the Manager's Website and increasing the numbers in the HR Shared Services Centre and up-skilling them.

A move to manager self-service is a big cultural change that must be managed effectively. An HR manager from the NHS suggested that while it needs to be explained to management that they should be responsible for their staff, it should also be explained to them that they are not expected to become HR managers.

> *We expect managers to manage their budget but not to be accountants. In the same way, we expect them to manage their staff, but not to be personnel professionals.*

The acceptance of this new role by managers demands effective change management and learning processes as well as role modelling by the senior management. In Nortel the European HR VP sets the example to fellow managers by logging onto the tool daily to check for notifications about approvals or to activate salary or position changes. The employees are engaged with the system by the need to request their holiday online, and the checking for approval notifications is very quickly becoming a core function of every employee's role within the company.

> 'The acceptance of [a] new role by managers demands effective change management and learning processes as well as role modelling by the senior management.'

TfL, however, has approached the introduction of the new technology and HR services in a different way. They believed that although there was room for improving the HR-to-employee ratio by reducing the HR headcount, they would not try to improve the efficiency of HR at the expense of the manager's effectiveness. Their HR community still has a significant role to play in helping the managers through the cultural and process changes. The reorganisation ensured that there were enough HR people remaining to help coach the managers through their new roles and help educate them in the new processes and technology.

In addition, the benefits to the organisation of the change in the managers' role must be explained and managers must be trained to understand the processes that they are required to perform and the technological systems that support these processes.

Increased availability of information

As has been suggested elsewhere in this report, the use of information technology within HR may result in an increased availability of information for managers through the HR intranet or electronic employee records. This is seen as a positive change by managers. Managers from Norwich Union were pleased that they could now look at information about their direct and indirect reports online. The availability of information on absence, for instance, allowed them to be more proactive in managing that information. This sentiment was echoed in several of the case studies. Indeed, the availability of information for managers may result in their being more engaged with their role and the organisation – provided that they understand the benefits and believe they have sufficient support.

SUMMARY

This chapter has examined the impact of technology in HR on the changing role of HR and other managers and has proposed that a reduction in the amount of administrative and transactional work expected of HR practitioners may allow more time for value-added work and facilitate a move towards the more strategic role of a business partner. It has also been noted that a number of organisations have introduced technology in HR in conjunction with a change in the structure of the HR function to that of using a shared services model. Finally, with regard to the HR role it is apparent that HR practitioners may be able to adopt a more advisory or strategic role due to the increased availability of reliable HR data.

The impact of technology in HR on other managers was investigated and it was suggested that the introduction of HR technology may result in increased responsibility for line managers in people management, and in conjunction with this, an increase in workload. Further it was emphasised that the use of technology in HR also meant that HR information was readily available to managers and HR business partners.

SUMMARY 7

This report has examined the use and impact of technology within the HR function. There is no doubt that the implementation of information technology within HR is a complex matter and that the requirements for the implementation and the impact of the technology differ according to the nature of the organisation and of the technology. However, there are a number of principles that hold true across organisations and technological solutions. This report has demonstrated that the implementation of technology within HR should not be taken lightly, and also that technology can have significant impacts on the efficiency of HR processes, employee engagement and communication and on the role and skills of HR and other managers.

Drawing on experience from ten case-study organisations from a range of industries within the private, public and not-for-profit sectors, this report identifies a number of effects that HRIS can have on the HR function and upon the wider organisation. It has endeavoured to suggest a number of areas of good practice in the development and implementation of technological systems in HR. While these are not intended to be an exhaustive list of the steps to take during the implementation process, they may be used to advise those organisations undertaking such an implementation. The conclusions drawn on the impact of technology in HR have implications for HR practice. These have been discussed in detail in the main body of the report and are summarised here.

THE USE AND IMPACT OF TECHNOLOGY IN HR

Planning for an e-HRM system

An examination of the case studies highlighted a number of issues on the development of information technology in HR. First, the production of an effective business case may be problematic. However, the introduction of technology in HR is usually driven by potential improvements such as in the speed and efficiency of processes, cost savings, increased accuracy of data, improved transparency and consistency of processes, increased availability of information and the facilitation of a change in the role of HRM. The business case may be strengthened by a business 'hook' or driver and by its alignment with the HR, business and IT strategies.

> 'The design of a system normally involves some trade-off between using the "vanilla" solution and customising it to fit with organisational needs.'

Consultation with potential users on the design and development of the system is essential in order to map out processes and to ensure that the system will be usable. Some attention should also be paid to managing the relationship between HR and IT. The design of a system normally involves some trade-off between using the 'vanilla' solution and customising the system to fit with organisational needs. This must be considered carefully, as should the branding of the solution, which should fit with the HR and organisational brand. Finally, extensive testing of the system with potential users is essential in order to produce a product that is usable and effective.

Obtaining stakeholder buy-in

Steps must be taken to engage users with the technology if its implementation is to be successful. Engagement processes should start as early as possible through the involvement of users in the development process. It is essential that communications with employees should be excellent throughout the development and implementation process so that they are well-informed and therefore more likely to accept the system. This may be achieved through the use of employee or senior management champions and user groups.

Education and tr
include an expla
technology and
system in a safe
systems and fee
engagement of u

Impact on t
processes

The use of techn
the efficient deliv
from the case stu
to HR processes
more transparent
these effects req
introduction of te
structure. Howev
accuracy and cos
should be noted
integration of the
in the wider orgar

Impact on e
communica

Evidence shows t
engagement, in tl
committed and m
communication b
managers and em
workforce is wide
intranet can mear
both managers ar
communication ca
practices such as
employee engage
electronic commu
employees and di
therefore importar
face-to-face conta

Impact on th
managers

> '...the abilit
> HRIS allows
> driven decis
> with consul

The use of technol
and skills of HR an
systems commonly
administrative and

REFERENCES AND FURTHER READING

CEDARCRESTONE (2006)

Workforce Technologies and Service Delivery Approaches Survey. www.cedarcrestone.com.

CIPD (2005)

People Management and Technology: Progress and potential. Survey. London, CIPD.

CIPD (2006)

HR and Technology: Beyond delivery. Change agenda. London, CIPD.

CIPD (2006)

The Changing HR Function: The key questions. Change agenda. London, CIPD.

CIPD (2006)

What's the Future for Human Capital? Executive briefing. London, CIPD.

CRANFIELD SCHOOL OF MANAGEMENT (2003)

Cranet Survey 2003. Human Resource Research Centre, Cranfield School of Management, UK.

ENSHUR, E., NIELSON, T. and GRANT-VALLONE, E. (2002)

'Tales from the hiring line: effects of the Internet and technology on HR processes', *Organizational Dynamics*, Vol. 31, No. 3: 224–44.

GUEST, D. and CONWAY, N. (2004)

Employee Well-being and the Psychological Contract. Research report. London, CIPD.

GUEUTAL, H. (2003)

'The brave new world of e-HR', in *Advances in Human Performance and Cognitive Engineering Research*, Vol. *3*. London, Elsevier Science Ltd.

KETTLEY, P. and O'REILLY, P. (2003)

E-HR: An introduction. Brighton, Institute of Employment Studies.

MARTIN, G. (2005)

Technology and People Management: The opportunity and the challenge. Research report. London, CIPD.

MARTINSONS, M. (1994)

'Benchmarking human resource information systems in Canada and Hong Kong', *Information and Management*, Vol. 26: 305–16.

MINISTRY OF MANPOWER, SINGAPORE (2003)

E-HR: Leveraging technology. Case study series 2/2003. Singapore, Ministry of Manpower.

REDDINGTON, M., WITHERS, M. and WILLIAMSON, M. (2005)

Transforming HR: Creating value through people. Oxford. Elsevier Butterworth-Heinemann.

SCOTT-JACKSON, W., NEWHAM, T. and GURNEY, M. (2005)

HR Outsourcing: The key decisions. Executive briefing. London, CIPD

SPARROW, P.R. (2005)

Internationa Recruitment, Selection and Assessment. Research report. London, CIPD

TANNENBAUM, S. (1990)

'HRIS: user group implications', *Journal of Systems Management*, Vol. 41, No. 1: 27–32.

TRUSS, C., SOANE, E., EDWARDS, C., WISDOM, K., CROLL, A. and BURNETT, J. (2006)

Working Life: Employee attitudes and engagement survey. Research report. London, CIPD.

ULRICH, D. (1997)

Human Resource Champions. Boston, Harvard Business School Press.

WATSON WYATT (2002)

B2E/EHR Survey results 2002. www.watsonwyatt.com.

WHITTINGTON, R. and MOLLOY, E. (2005)

HR's role in Organising: Shaping change. Research report. London, CIPD.

Note: CIPD published products are available from the CIPD website: www.cipd.co.uk